From Your Friends at The MAILBOX®

Environment

Grades 1–3

INVESTIGATING SCIENCE

Project Manager:
Thad H. McLaurin

Writer:
Beth A. Miller

Editors:
Deborah T. Kalwat, Scott Lyons, Jennifer Munnerlyn,
Hope H. Taylor

Art Coordinator:
Clevell Harris

Artists:
Susan Hodnett, Sheila Krill, Rob Mayworth,
Greg D. Rieves, Rebecca Saunders

Cover Artists:
Nick Greenwood and Kimberly Richard

D1297754

www.themailbox.com

©2000 by THE EDUCATION CENTER, INC.
All rights reserved.
ISBN #1-56234-366-1

Manufactured in the United States

10 9 8 7 6 5 4 3 2 1

Table of Contents

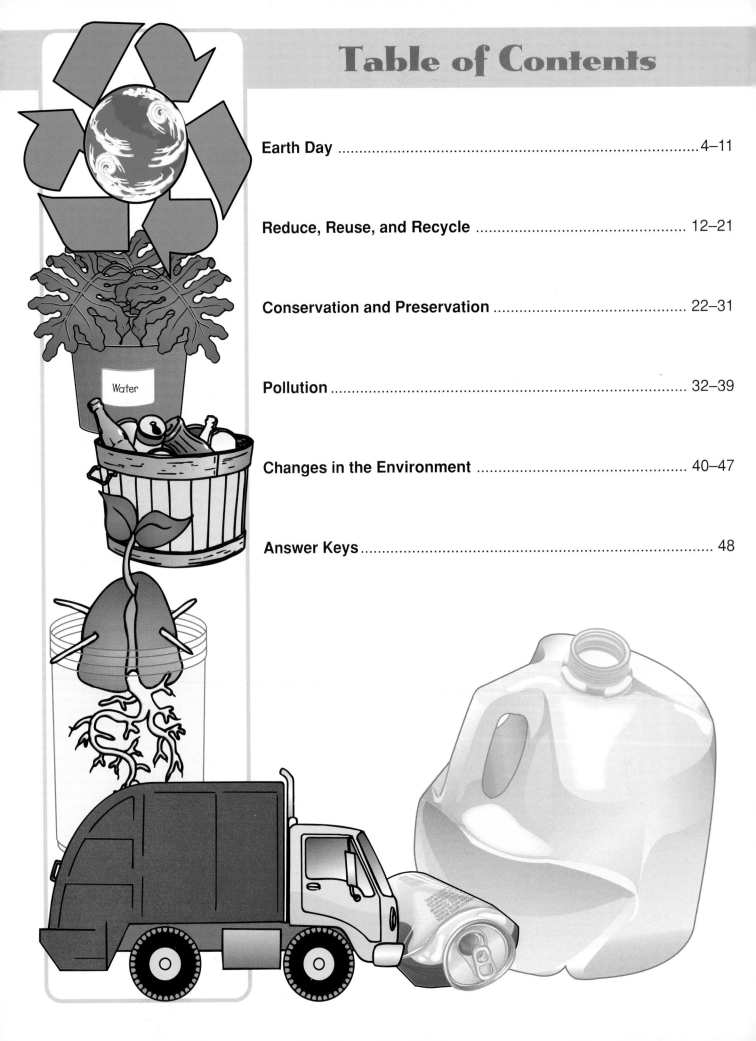

About This Book

Welcome to *Investigating Science—Environment*! This book is one of ten must-have resource books that support the National Science Education Standards and are designed to supplement and enhance your existing science curriculum. Packed with practical cross-curricular ideas and thought-provoking reproducibles, these all-new, content-specific resource books provide primary teachers with a collection of innovative and fun activities for teaching thematic science units.

Included in this book:
Investigating Science—Environment contains five cross-curricular thematic units, each containing
- Background information for the teacher
- Easy-to-implement instructions for science experiments and projects
- Student-centered activities and reproducibles
- Literature links

Cross-curricular thematic units found in this book:
- *Earth Day*
- *Reduce, Reuse, and Recycle*
- *Conservation and Preservation*
- *Pollution*
- *Changes in the Environment*

Other books in the primary Investigating Science series:
- *Investigating Science—Amphibians & Reptiles*
- *Investigating Science—Insects*
- *Investigating Science—Solar System*
- *Investigating Science—Plants*
- *Investigating Science—Energy*
- *Investigating Science—Mammals*
- *Investigating Science—Weather*
- *Investigating Science—Rocks & Minerals*
- *Investigating Science—Health & Safety*

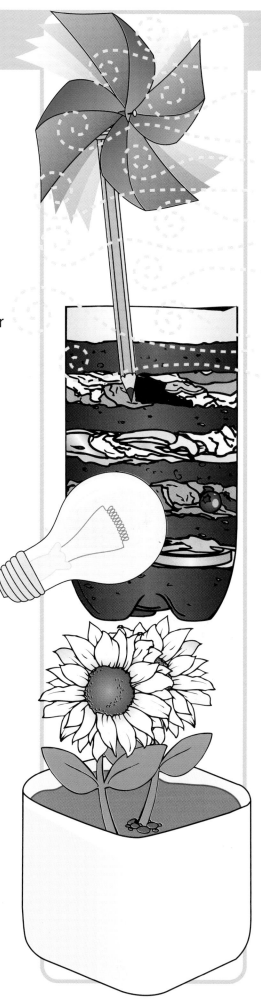

Earth Day

Stimulate your students' interest in Earth Day and build global awareness with this collection of activities, experiments, and reproducibles.

Global Vision
(Critical Thinking, Art)

Use this worldly mobile-making activity to showcase your students' visions for the planet. Provide three small paper plates, crayons, and a length of yarn for each student. Next, display a world map so that it is visible to all students.

Then instruct each child to draw and color continents and oceans on the front and back of one paper plate to resemble the earth. On the front of the second plate, have the child draw and color a scene, such as a field or a beach, that is polluted and dirty. On the back of the second plate, have him draw the same scene without the pollution. Finally, direct the child to program the front and back of the third plate with a message about his vision for the planet. To assemble the mobile, have the student hole-punch the top and bottom of the first two plates and the top of the third plate. Then instruct the student to use the length of yarn to connect the plates as shown. Suspend the completed mobiles in the classroom for a breezy celebration of Earth Day.

My vision
for the
planet...

Charles

Background for the Teacher

- Earth Day is celebrated on April 22.
- The first Earth Day was observed on April 22, 1970.
- It takes 150 pounds of recycled paper to save one tree.
- A leaking toilet can lose over 22,000 gallons of water in one year.
- A five-minute shower uses about 25 gallons of water.
- If you took all of the Styrofoam® cups that are manufactured in one day and lined them up end to end, they would go all the way around the planet.

Reading to Save the Planet

Celebrating Earth Day (Circle the Year With Holidays Series) by Janet McDonnell (Children's Press, 1994)

Dear Children of the Earth by Schim Schimmel (NorthWord Press, 1994)

Earth Day by Linda Lowery (First Avenue Editions, 1992)

Fifty Simple Things Kids Can Do to Save the Earth by Earthworks Group (Andrews McMeel Publishing, 1990)

The Great Kapok Tree: A Tale of the Amazon Rain Forest by Lynne Cherry (Harcourt Brace & Company, 1990)

Good as New!
(Community Service Project)

Finding new homes for toys that are no longer in use provides a great opportunity for teaching students another method of recycling! A few weeks before Earth Day, ask students to begin collecting toys and games that they have outgrown or no longer care for and bring them to school. (Remind youngsters to obtain parent permission before they bring a toy to school.)

To prepare the toys for a new owner, set up a "good as new" center with sponges, mild detergents, water, and masking tape. Invite each student to visit the center and use the materials to wash and repair the toys that she is donating.

Ask the class to brainstorm a list of possible donation places for the toys. Encourage them to think of local children's charities or a younger classroom that would benefit from receiving the toys. Have the class vote to determine where the donation will be made and arrange to have the toys delivered on or near Earth Day. Now this activity really helps children understand that everything old is new again!

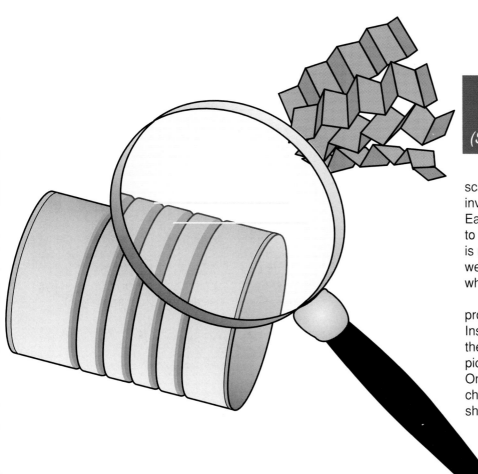

Environment Detectives
(Scavenger Hunt, Critical Thinking)

Sending students on an Earth Day scavenger hunt is sure to inspire them to investigate the world around them. On Earth Day, take the class to the playground to complete the activity. If an outdoor area is not available, or in case of inclement weather, students can complete the activity while looking out a window.

Have each child choose a partner, and provide a copy of page 9 for each pair. Instruct the twosome to look at the things in their environment and draw an appropriate picture for each statement on the sheet. Once the sheets are completed, gather the children in a circle and invite each pair to share its findings with the rest of the class.

It's in the Bag!
(Recycling, Community Involvement, Art)

What's the best way to advertise Earth Day within your community? Get your local grocery store involved! For information about The Earth Day Groceries Project, 2000, visit the Web site (http://www.earthdaybags.org/). To get your class involved, tell the store manager about the project and ask her for a class supply of paper grocery bags. Have students use crayons and markers to decorate the bags with environmental messages and illustrations. Return the bags to the store and ask the manager to use the bags for customers' groceries on Earth Day. Now that's a great way for students to spread the word about Earth Day!

Earth Day Heroes
(Writing, Self-Esteem)

Understanding that they can play a part in saving the planet will make your students feel like heroes! Use the following bookmaking activity to help your students tell others about their heroics. Prepare for the lesson by sharing *Taking Care of the Earth: Kids in Action* by Laurence Pringle (Boyds Mills Press, 1997). Next, have students brainstorm ideas about the things they can do to make a difference, and list their suggestions on chart paper. Then distribute a sheet of white construction paper and crayons to each student. Have her use the ideas from the brainstormed list to write and illustrate a sentence about what she can do to help save the planet. Bind the completed pages into a book titled "Earth Day Heroes." (If desired, laminate the pages for durability before binding.) Read the book to the class before placing it in the class library.

Earth Day Sing-Along
(Song)

Have students join you in this song about the earth!

This Earth Is Your Earth
(sung to the tune of "This Land Is Your Land")
This earth is your earth.
This earth is my earth.
And we can all help
To preserve its worth.
We can recycle
And pick up litter.
Keep this earth clean for you and me.

When I see trees grow,
I smile, for I know
They make the air clean,
And keep the world green.
So when it's Earth Day,
I cheer and I say,
Keep this earth clean for you and me.

"Tree-rific" Plant
(Planting a Tree)

An avocado seed, a few toothpicks, and a jar of water are the only props you need for this "tree-mendous" lesson. Gather the needed materials. (It's best to use a seed from an avocado that has never been refrigerated.) Then stick the toothpicks in the seed as shown and suspend the seed in the jar. Fill the jar with enough water to cover the bottom third of the seed; then place the jar near a sunny window. Assign different students to refill the jar with water as needed.

Once the seed has sprouted, it will be ready to plant. Fill a large pot with soil. Dig a small hole in the middle of the soil and carefully place the seed, roots down, in the hole. Gently cover the seed so that the "tree" is showing; then place the pot in a sunny spot. Culminate the activity by gathering students around the tree and reading *Button, Bucket, Sky* by Jacqueline Briggs Martin (Carolrhoda Books, 1998).

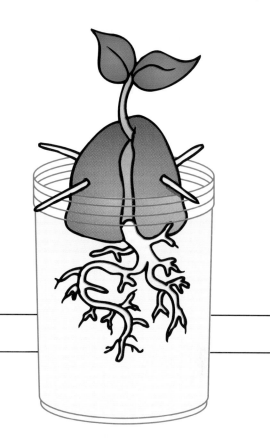

Acid Rain Effects
(Science Experiment)

Acid rain occurs when rain mixes with gases in the atmosphere. These gases can come from factories, car exhausts, forest fires, and other sources. Acid rain can kill or damage trees, plants, and animals. Give your students firsthand experience with the effects of acid rain with the following experiment.

Obtain two small plants that are as similar as possible, two small spray bottles, and a bottle of white vinegar. Fill one bottle with water and the other bottle with a mixture of half vinegar and half water. Label the bottles carefully. Use sticky notes to label one plant "water" and one plant "acid rain." Then place the plants on a sunny windowsill. Give each student a copy of page 10 and have him draw a picture of each plant at the beginning of the experiment.

Each day, assign a different child to mist the "water" plant with water and the "acid rain" plant with the vinegar mixture. Encourage each student to examine the plants weekly and record any changes by illustrating them on his sheet. Within two weeks, the "acid rain" plant's leaves should begin to turn yellow and fall off. Eventually, the plant will die. This happens because most plants cannot survive when the acid level in their water is high. Discuss the results of the experiment with the class.

Water

Water

Acid Rain

Acid Rain

Earthdance
(Writing Poetry, Listening)

The beauty of the earth is poetically described in the book *Earthdance* by Joanne Ryder (Henry Holt and Company, 1999). After reading the book aloud, ask your students to close their eyes as you reread the book. Encourage them to use their imaginations as the words invite them to "be" the planet.

Use the text as an inspiration for this creative-writing activity. Divide the class into five teams of equal size and assign each team one of the five senses: sight, hearing, taste, smell, or touch. Give each team a sheet of chart paper and a marker. Then ask the team members to brainstorm a list of the things on the earth that they can experience through the assigned sense. Post the completed lists around the classroom.

Next, give each student a copy of page 11. Instruct her to use the lists to write a five-senses poem about the earth. After completing the poem, have her color it lightly and cut out the earth. Post the poems on a bulletin board titled "A World of Poetry."

Sight – Beautiful sunset

Hearing – Birds singing

Taste – Fresh vegetables from the garden

Smell – Spring morning

Touch – Dew on the grass

Happy Earth Day to You!
(Celebration)

What's the best way to celebrate everything that you've learned about saving the planet? Have an Earth Day party! Before the party, enlist students' help with some earth-friendly decorations. Follow the directions below to prepare.

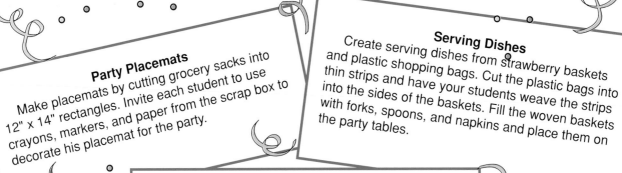

Party Placemats
Make placemats by cutting grocery sacks into 12" x 14" rectangles. Invite each student to use crayons, markers, and paper from the scrap box to decorate his placemat for the party.

Serving Dishes
Create serving dishes from strawberry baskets and plastic shopping bags. Cut the plastic bags into thin strips and have your students weave the strips into the sides of the baskets. Fill the woven baskets with forks, spoons, and napkins and place them on the party tables.

Earth Day Treats
For an Earth Day treat, bake a layer cake according to box directions and let the layers cool. Spread white frosting between the layers and on the sides of the cake, reserving some frosting for the top. Add a few drops of blue food coloring to the remaining frosting and mix it thoroughly. Spread the blue frosting over the top of the cake. Mix shredded coconut and several drops of green food coloring together in a bowl and sprinkle the green coconut on the top of the cake in shapes that resemble continents. Serve slices of the cake with blue or green punch.

Be an Environment Detective!

I see one thing that needs clean air to breathe.

I see one thing that needs clean water.

I see one place where people might litter.

I see one thing that produces air pollution.

Bonus Box: On the back of this sheet, draw two more things that you see in your environment.

Note to the teacher: Use with "Environment Detectives" on page 5.

9

Acid Rain Effects

	Day One	Week Two	Week Three	Week Four	Week Five

	Day One	Week Two	Week Three	Week Four	Week Five

What did you learn about acid rain? _____

_____

_____

Bonus Box: On a separate sheet of paper, write a letter to a friend describing the acid rain experiment.

Note to the teacher: Use with "Acid Rain Effects" on page 7.

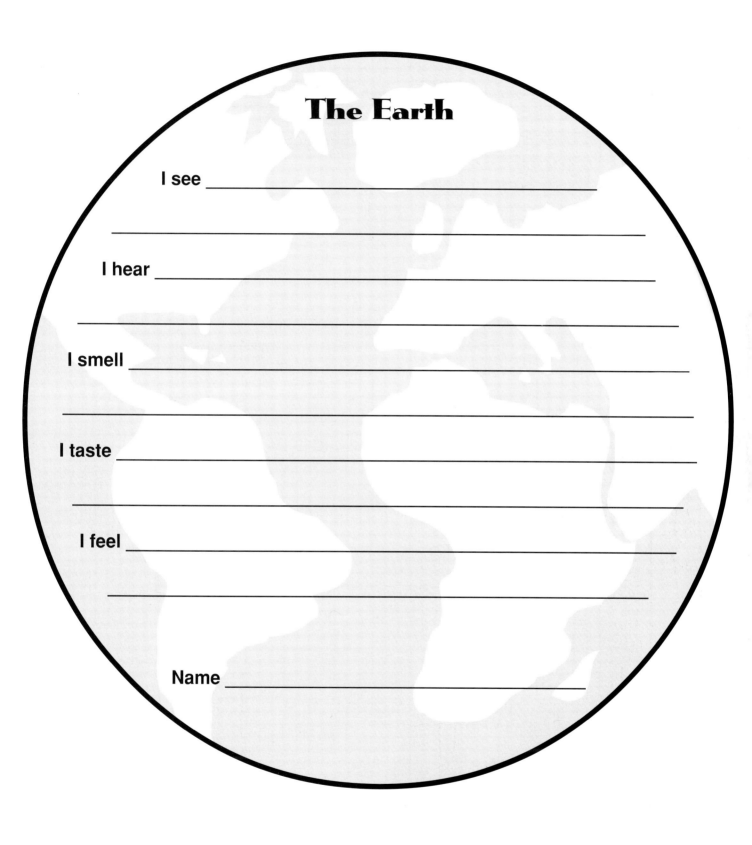

The Earth

I see _____

_____

I hear _____

_____

I smell _____

_____

I taste _____

_____

I feel _____

_____

Name _____

Reduce, Reuse, and Recycle

Use this collection of activities to teach your students about the three Rs—Reduce, Reuse, and Recycle—and help make the earth a healthier, cleaner planet.

Background for the Teacher

- *Reduce*—to create less waste.
- *Reuse*—to use the same item again or to use an old product for a new purpose.
- *Recycle*—to use the material of an old product to make a new product instead of throwing it away.
- The average American produces about more than three pounds of trash every day.
- Common recyclable materials include aluminum and steel cans, glass containers, plastic, and paper.
- Recycling conserves raw materials needed by manufacturers.
- Recycling reduces the pollution that may result from disposing of waste material.
- Recyclable materials have the most value when they're not mixed in with the rest of your garbage. Separating your trash saves the expense of using special equipment to separate the recyclables from the nonrecyclables.
- *Composting*—a process of letting collected organic waste (yard and food waste) decompose into a substance that can be used for fertilizer.

Begin With the Basics— The Three Rs
(Bookmaking, Research)

Create awareness of the basics of recycling by first teaching your students the three Rs—*reduce, reuse,* and *recycle.* Begin by explaining to your students the difference between reducing, reusing, and recycling (see Background for the Teacher). Tell your students that they are going to create their own picture booklets about the three Rs. Give each student a copy of pages 17 and 18. Also give each student crayons and scissors. Instruct the student to write definitions for *reduce, reuse,* and *recycle* on the appropriate booklet pages. Then have the student draw an illustration for each term. Instruct each student to cut the booklet pages apart along the bold lines, stack them in order with the cover on top, and staple the booklets together as shown. Encourage your students to take their booklets home to share with their parents.

Reading Is Recyclable!

Fifty Simple Things Kids Can Do to Save the Earth by The Earthworks Group (Andrews McMeel Publishing, 1990)

Gardens From Garbage: How to Grow Indoor Plants From Recycled Kitchen Scraps by Judith F. Handelsman (The Millbrook Press, Inc.; 1994)

The Great Trash Bash by Loreen Leedy (Holiday House, Inc.; 1991)

Waste, Recycling and Re-Use (Protecting Our Planet series) by Steve Parker (Raintree Steck-Vaughn Publishers, 1998)

The Wump World by Bill Peet (Houghton Mifflin Company, 1981)

From Trash to Treasure
(Arts and Crafts, Creative Thinking)

Tap into your students' creativity with this gem of an activity! Have your students bring in one dry trash item from home. Then instruct them to use their imaginations to come up with ideas to make something different and useful from their objects. For example, an old glass jar can be decorated and used as a pencil holder and a milk jug can be transformed into a planter. Give students time to work on their projects. Once completed, have each student explain to the class how she came up with the idea for her project and what treasure she made from her trash. Display the projects in your classroom or the library for all to see and enjoy.

Tons of Trash!
(Experiment)

Did you know that each person in the United States produces more than three pounds of garbage each day? Increase your students' understanding of just how much trash they produce by having a trash weigh-in. Give each student a large paper bag to collect all his dry, *inorganic* (no food!) trash for a day. Have each student write his name on his bag. During school, have him place the bag near his desk to collect his trash items throughout the day. At the end of the day, send the bag home with the student to continue collecting trash until bedtime. The following day, weigh each student's bag of trash on a scale. Next, give each student a copy of page 19. Then have the student fill in the first column of the reproducible with the weight of his trash. Ask students to share whether the collected garbage weighed more than they expected or less. As a group, talk about how to estimate the weight of the trash for one week and one month. Guide the students to use the estimates to complete the rest of the bar graph on page 19. Then read aloud the "Bonus Box" at the bottom of page 19. Help each student figure out how much trash he might throw away in one year. Next, discuss with the class the weight of the entire class's trash and remind the students how much more their trash would weigh if all the food that they threw away were included. Using page 19 as a guide, make a large graph of the entire class's trash and label it "Tons of Trash!"

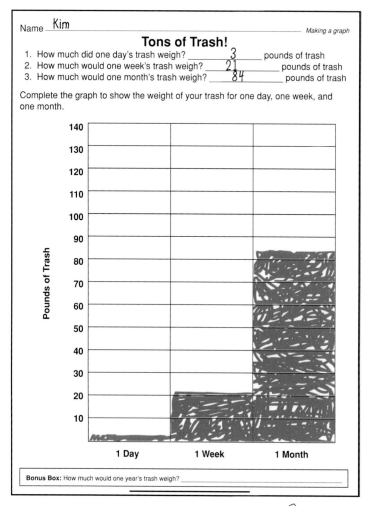

Name _Kim_ _____ *Making a graph*

Tons of Trash!

1. How much did one day's trash weigh? ____3____ pounds of trash
2. How much would one week's trash weigh? ____21____ pounds of trash
3. How much would one month's trash weigh? ____84____ pounds of trash

Complete the graph to show the weight of your trash for one day, one week, and one month.

Bonus Box: How much would one year's trash weigh? _____

Where Does the Trash Go?
(Creative Writing)

Where exactly does all the garbage go once it's collected? Use the following activity to help students better understand what happens to nonrecyclable trash. Read aloud *Where Does the Garbage Go?* by Paul Showers (HarperCollins Children's Books, 1994). Then use the book to review the function of the landfill with your class.

Next, have each student pretend to be a nonrecyclable piece of trash, such as an empty food container or a candy wrapper. Then instruct each student to write a story about what happens to the piece of trash (from the trash's point of view) from the time it is thrown away and transported to the landfill. Remind each student to tell what means of transportation he used to reach his destination, what happened along the way, and what he discovered there. Bind together each student's adventure into a class book titled "Where Does the Trash Go?"

Two-Liter Landfills
(Experiment)

What better way is there for your students to see a landfill in action than by having them create their own? Ahead of time, collect the materials listed below. Then divide your students into pairs and guide each pair in following the directions below to create a two-liter landfill.

After the four-week observation period is over, discuss with students which items decayed in their landfills and which items did not. Ask your students what they think happens to the trash items that don't decay in a real landfill. Then discuss why it is important to reduce, reuse, and recycle.

Materials for each pair: one 2-liter bottle with the top cut off; 1 permanent marker; soil; garbage items, such as food scraps (no meat), plastic, paper, and foil; 1 copy of page 20

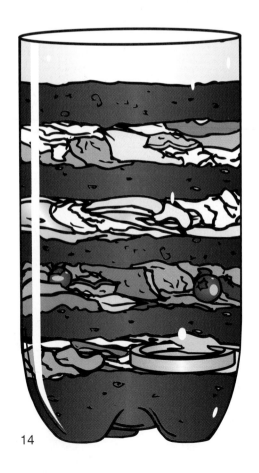

Steps:
1. Write your name on the bottom of the bottle.
2. Fill the bottom of the bottle with a layer of soil.
3. Place a layer of one type of trash on top of the soil.
4. Place a layer of soil on top of the trash layer. Repeat this process with a different type of trash layer until there are four to five layers of trash.
5. Place the landfill in a sunny location. Water it daily to keep it moist.
6. On page 20, draw an illustration of the landfill after one week. Then write underneath the illustration a brief description of the landfill and how it's changed.
7. Continue to water the landfill and observe the changes that take place.
8. Draw an illustration of the landfill after four weeks. Then write underneath the illustration a brief description of the landfill and how it's changed.

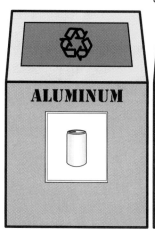

Recycling to the Rescue
(Reading, Sorting)

To further explain the concept of recycling, read *Recycle! A Handbook for Kids* by Gail Gibbons (Little, Brown and Company; 1996). Discuss with your students the different kinds of recyclable materials—such as paper, glass, aluminum, and plastic—and the importance of separating them from nonreclyclable trash. Explain that recycling helps protect and save the earth's natural resources. To check for understanding of the various types of recyclables, give each student a copy of page 21 to complete as directed. Also supply each student with scissors and glue.

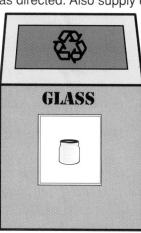

ALUMINUM

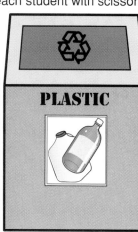

GLASS

PLASTIC

PAPER

Junk Mail Jamboree
(Experiment)

One way to reduce the large amount of trash that is thrown away is to eliminate junk mail. How much junk mail do your students' families receive each day, each week, or each month? Find out with a junk mail jamboree! A few days in advance, send a note home explaining to parents that your class will be collecting junk mail. Ask them to send any appropriate junk mail to school with their child daily for one week. Place several junk mail collection boxes near the door of the classroom. At the end of the week, weigh the junk mail for a grand total. Based on the junk mail's total weight, help your students figure out how much the junk mail would weigh if collected for one month and then for one year. Brainstorm solutions for cutting down on junk mail and what to do with it once you have it. Solutions might include using the junk mail to make your own paper.

Junk Mail

Plastic Milk Jug

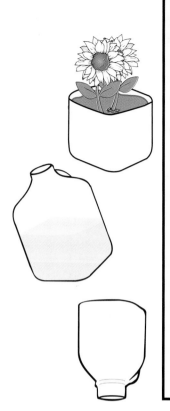

—planter

—watering jug

—funnel (cut the bottom off)

Don't Lose It—Reuse It
(Critical Thinking)

Challenge your students to think of different ways to reuse items instead of throwing them away. List each of the following items on separate sheets of chart paper: shoebox, plastic milk jug, glass jar, wooden board, plastic bag, newspaper, coffee can, cardboard paper-towel tube. Have each student select two items listed on the chart paper. Then have the student think of three ways each of the selected items can be reused. Encourage students to think of ideas that are practical and/or creative. Then call on each student to share his ideas for how to reuse the items he selected. Record the ideas on the appropriate charts. Continue until you have several ideas recorded on each chart. Keep the charts posted around the classroom during your study of the environment for students to refer to when considering how to reuse an item.

Pack It In!
(Critical Thinking)

Explore waste from everyday packaging materials—starting with students' lunches! Sandwich bags, plastic wrap, and juice boxes are common packaging materials in lunches. Explain to students that some materials are too complex to be recycled—juice boxes are made of a layer of plastic, a layer of paperboard, and a layer of aluminum foil stuck together. Further explain that since these materials can't be separated, the juice boxes can't be recycled and over 4 billion juice boxes are put into the trash every year!

Ahead of time, select a day to request that each child bring her lunch to school. Before students go to lunch, ask them to get out their lunches and examine the different kinds of packaging materials. Have them make a list of which items can be recycled or reused and which items cannot. Brainstorm with your students ways to repackage the lunches to reduce waste. Discuss the importance of packing food in recyclable or reusable packaging. Then have students ask their parents to try to pack "no waste" lunches. As an extension, encourage students to design environmentally friendly food product packaging by drawing pictures or constructing models.

Reduce, Reuse, and Recycle

by _____

©2000 The Education Center, Inc. • *Investigating Science* • Environment • TEC1739

Reduce

_____

_____

1

Book Patterns
Use with "Begin With the Basics—The Three Rs" on page 12.

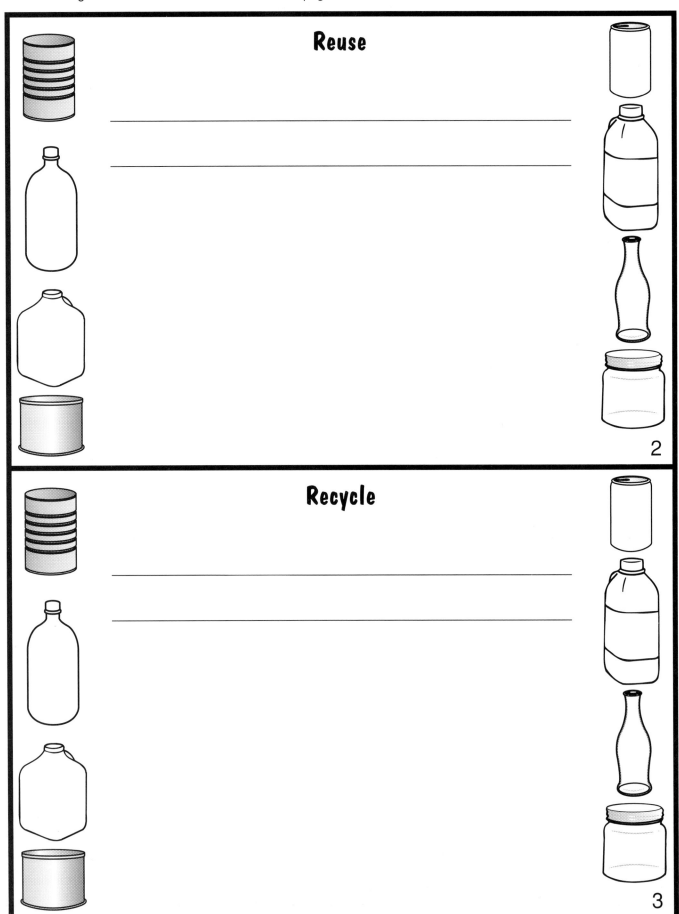

Reuse

2

Recycle

3

Tons of Trash!

1. How much did one day's trash weigh? _____ pounds of trash
2. How much would one week's trash weigh? _____ pounds of trash
3. How much would one month's trash weigh? _____ pounds of trash

Complete the graph to show the weight of your trash for one day, one week, and one month.

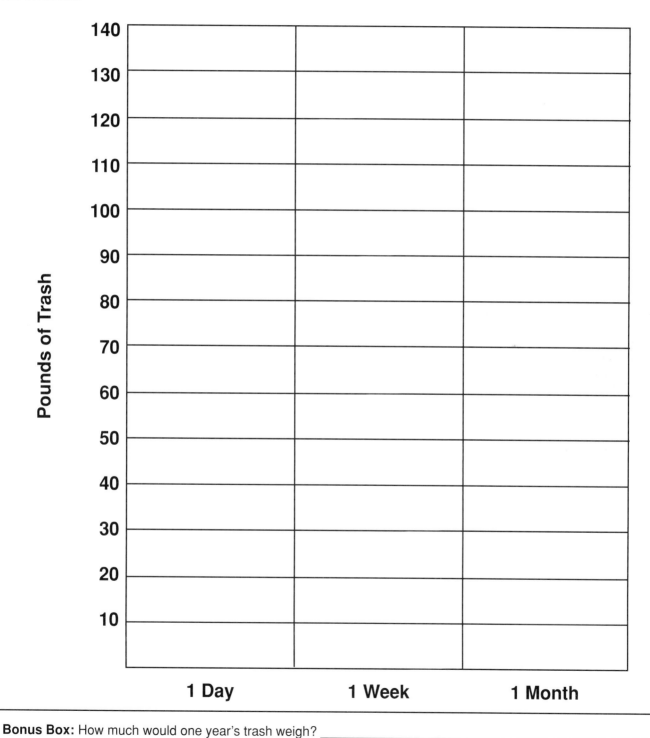

Bonus Box: How much would one year's trash weigh? _____

Note to the teacher: Use with "Tons of Trash!" on page 13.

Two-Liter Landfills

Week 1

Week 4

After one week our landfill...

After four weeks our landfill...

_____

_____

_____

_____

_____

_____

_____

_____

_____

_____

_____

_____

Sorting

Putting Trash in Its Place

Cut out the boxes below.
Sort the boxes by recycling material.
Glue each box onto the correct bin.

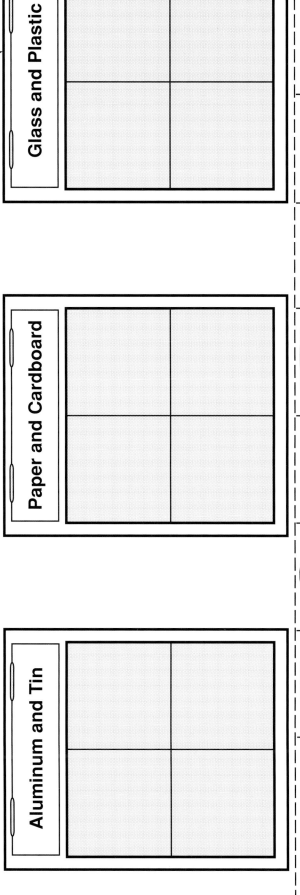

Glass and Plastic

Paper and Cardboard

Aluminum and Tin

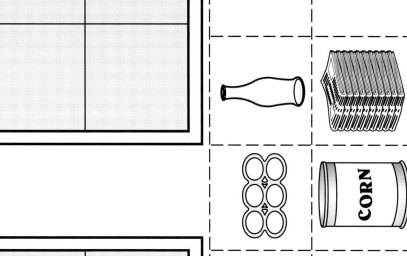

©2000 The Education Center, Inc. • *Investigating Science • Environment* • TEC1739 • Key p. 48

Note to the teacher: Use with "Recycling to the Rescue" on page 15.

21

Conservation and Preservation

Get your students involved in preserving and conserving the earth's natural resources with this collection of ready-to-go activities!

To Conserve or Preserve?
(Critical Thinking, Writing)

Help your students understand the difference between conservation and preservation with this engaging activity. Gather ahead of time a jam jar and an empty, clean paper quart-sized beverage carton. Use a clothespin to fasten the carton closed as shown. Label the carton "Conserve" and the jam jar "Preserve." Explain to your students that *conservation* is the use of natural resources in a planned and careful way and that *preservation* is keeping natural resources as safe and untouched as possible. Next, have students help you list natural resources that they believe should be conserved or preserved. Then have each student record, on two separate slips of paper, a natural resource in her community or state that she believes should be conserved, and one that should be preserved. Allow each student to share her natural resource choices with the class, before folding and depositing each slip into the Preserve jar or the Conserve carton. Throughout the unit, pull a different slip from each container, and read it aloud to the class. Direct the students to write a brief paragraph explaining why it is important to preserve or conserve that natural resource.

Background for the Teacher

- *Conservation* is the wise use of the land and its natural resources in order to prevent abuse, ruin, or disregard.
- *Preservation* is the act of preserving, or keeping intact, the land and its natural resources.
- Rain forests are located along the equator, in Central Africa, in Southeast Asia, and in Central and South America.
- Rain forests cover less than 10% of the earth's land, but contain around 60% of all the plant and animal species on the earth.
- Each year, nearly 50 million acres of tropical rain forests are burned or cleared.
- About 850 tree species are native to the United States. There are no federal laws that protect endangered forests in the United States.
- Each year, 78 million tons of paper products are produced from trees.
- Only 5% of the earth's population lives in the United States, but the United States uses 34% of the earth's energy.
- One load of laundry can use up to 50 gallons of water.

Planet-Friendly Booklist

Aani and the Tree Huggers by Jeannine Atkins (Lee & Low Books Inc., 1995)
Common Ground: The Water, Earth, and Air We Share by Molly Bang (Scholastic Inc., 1997)
Look Closer: Rain Forest by Barbara Taylor, Frank Greenaway, and Deni Brown (Dorling Kindersley Publishing, Inc.; 1998)
Parks Are to Share (Building Block Books) by Lee Sullivan Hill (Carolrhoda Books, Inc.; 1997)
Song for the Ancient Forest by Nancy Luenn (Atheneum, 1993)

A Day in the Life
(Reading, Letter Writing)

Introduce your students to the unique creatures living in the rain forest by reading *The Great Kapok Tree* by Lynne Cherry (Harcourt Brace, 1998). After reading the story, make a class chart listing the animals and each animal's reason for saving the kapok tree. Then assign each student an animal from the book and instruct him to write about a typical day in the rain forest from his animal's point of view. Provide library books or other reference materials, and crayons or markers to help each student illustrate his animal tale. Together with students, write a brief letter to your state senator or congressman, sharing the information students have learned from the book and encouraging the official(s) to pass laws to protect endangered forests around the world. Finally, send the letter along with your students' animal tales to the following addresses:

Congressman/woman _____
U.S. House of Representatives
Washington, DC 20515

Senator _____
U.S. Senate
Washington, DC 20510

Note: Check out *www.friend.ly.net/scoop/biographies/ cherrylynne/index.html* for more information about Lynne Cherry and her involvement in rain forest preservation. *(Current as of 1/00.)*

The Great Kapok Tree

Animal:	Animal's reason for saving the tree:
Boa constrictor	The tree is his home.
Bee	He comes to the tree to collect pollen.
Monkey	The tree holds the dirt in place.
Toucan, Macaw, and Cock-of-the-rock	The forest will disappear if the trees are cut down.
Tree frog	Without the tree he will be homeless.
Jaguar	Animals living in trees provide his food.
Porcupine	Trees produce oxygen.
Anteater	He doesn't want to live in a world without trees.
Three-toed sloth	The rain forest is too beautiful to chop down.

Rain Forest Mix

Mix together in a large container:

2 c. peanuts
2 c. chocolate chips
2 c. cashew nuts
2 c. dried banana chips
2 c. dried papaya
2 c. Brazil and/or macadamia nuts
2 c. coconut flakes

(Makes 56 ¼-cup servings)

Rain Forest Fund Raiser
(Class Fund-Raiser Project, Recipe)

Enjoy a taste of the tropics while earning money for a good cause! Ahead of time, obtain permission to set up a "Save the Rain Forest" fund-raising stand in the cafeteria. Then, as a class, prepare the Rain Forest Mix recipe (see left). Have students use permanent markers to decorate small plastic zippered bags with rain forest scenes. Fill each bag with one-fourth cup of the Rain Forest Mix. Have students sell the Rain Forest Mix at the designated fund-raiser stand during lunch. Then use your earnings to protect a part of the rain forest in your class's name by sending a $25 donation to Rainforest Action Network Protect-an-Acre, 221 Pine St. #500, San Francisco, CA 94104. The Rainforest Action Network will send your students a Protect-an-Acre certificate thanking them for helping preserve rain forest land.

TRASH

Adopt-a-Playground
Pine Elementary
(Mrs. Smith's class)

Keep It Clean!

laminated recycled paper

piece of wood

coffee can filled with dirt or sand

Adopt a Playground
(Community Service Project)

Give your students hands-on practice caring for an environment they cherish—their school playground! To begin, take your students on a short walking tour of the playground or another school area. Have students bring clipboards or notepads so they can record or sketch their observations of the area. Return to the classroom and have students share some of the problems they noticed with the playground—litter, damaged equipment, erosion, no grass, etc. Then help the students brainstorm ways to improve the playground. (For example: pick up trash, plant flowers, put out more trash cans, etc.) Have the students vote on the top three improvements they want to implement. Post an Adopt-a-Playground sign on your playground similar to the one shown, and follow through with some of the students' beautification ideas. Involve other teachers and classes by assigning each class a different month in which to act as the Adopt-a-Playground sponsor.

National Treasures
(Song, Mapmaking)

Help develop an appreciation for our national treasures—the national parks—with this fun, informational song. Then have students create their own national parks with the mapmaking reproducible on page 28.

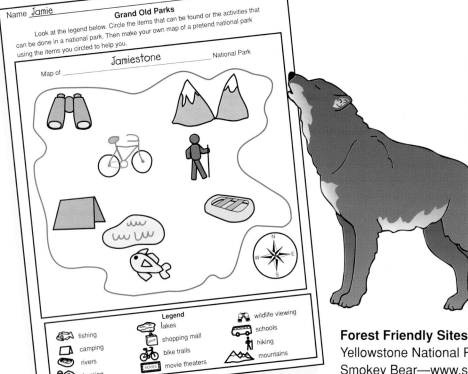

Name Jamie   Mapmaking
Grand Old Parks
Look at the legend below. Circle the items that can be found or the activities that can be done in a national park. Then make your own map of a pretend national park using the items you circled to help you.

Map of ___ Jamiestone ___ National Park

Legend
- fishing
- camping
- rivers
- farming
- lakes
- shopping mall
- bike trails
- movie theaters
- wildlife viewing
- schools
- hiking
- mountains

(sung to the tune of "On Top of Old Smokey")

In the middle of Yellowstone,
Our first national park,
The trees are protected,
Their leaves, roots, and bark.

You shouldn't pick flowers,
Or leave any litter.
So the lakes will all stay clean,
And they'll sparkle like glitter.

The wolves have a home there,
And so do the bears.
The steam from Old Faithful
Shoots into the air.

Come visit Yellowstone,
Our first national park,
Where the trees are protected,
Their leaves, roots, and bark.

Forest Friendly Sites: *(Current as of 1/00.)*
Yellowstone National Park—www.nps.gov/yell/index.htm
Smokey Bear—www.smokeybear.com
Woodsy Owl—www.fs.fed.us/spf/woodsy

Animal Friends
(Creative Writing, Art, Game)

Make your students aware of animal rights with this creative-writing idea. Begin by explaining to students that many plants and animals have become *extinct,* or no longer exist, because their homes were destroyed. Further explain that some animals are considered *endangered* because there are only a few thousand or fewer left. Then have each student draw a picture of his favorite wild animal and write a few sentences describing what the world would be like without this creature. Display the students' work on a bulletin board titled "Animal Friends."

To further extend this activity, pair students; then give each pair a copy of the game "Be Animal Friendly" (page 29), a copy of the cube pattern (page 30), glue, and scissors. Next, guide each pair through the directions on page 30 for making the cube. Then have the pair play the game as directed on page 29. For an added treat, provide the pairs with animal crackers to use as game pieces.

Fishing Trip Script

Blue Bowl Sea
Trip One:
1. Start with 30 fish.
2. Catch five.
3. Twenty-five fish are left in the sea—five groups of five.
4. Put in five new fish.

Trip Two:
1. Start with 30 fish.
2. Catch five.
3. Twenty-five fish are left in the sea—five groups of five.
4. Put in five new fish.

Red Bowl Sea
Trip One:
1. Start with 30 fish.
2. Catch ten.
3. Twenty fish are left in the sea—four groups of five.
4. Put in four new fish.

Trip Two:
1. Start with 24 fish.
2. Catch ten.
3. Fourteen fish are left in the sea—two groups of five.
4. Put in two new fish.

Trip Three:
1. Start with 16 fish.
2. Catch ten.
3. Six fish are left in the sea—one group of five.
4. Put in one new fish.

Trip Four:
1. Start with seven fish.
2. Catch seven.
3. There are no fish left.

Uh-oh! Overfishing
(Experiment, Math)

Clue students in to the consequences of overfishing our lakes, streams, and oceans with this yummy activity. Begin by pairing students. Next, give half the pairs each a red plastic bowl. Then give each remaining pair a blue plastic bowl. Supply every pair with a small condiment cup, a spoon, and 30 Goldfish® crackers. Explain that the pairs with blue bowls represent responsible fishing (catching five fish per fishing trip) and pairs with red bowls represent overfishing (catching ten fish per fishing trip). Display a transparency of the "Fishing Trip Script" (see left). Help your students navigate the steps by reading each step aloud. Have the students within each pair take turns catching the allotted amount of fish with the spoon, then storing the fish in the condiment cup until the end of the activity. After each fishing trip, have the pairs group their remaining fish into groups of five, as you distribute one cracker for every group of five fish remaining in each sea. Allow the pairs to fish until the Red Bowl Sea is empty. (The Blue Bowl Sea will always keep 30 fish due to responsible fishing.) Discuss with students the effects of overfishing while they enjoy eating their fish crackers.

Energy Officers
(Energy Awareness Activity)

Conserving energy is everyone's job. Motivate your youngsters to become more energy conscious with this activity. Make a list on chart paper as students brainstorm ways energy is wasted at home and at school. Next, duplicate the Energy Police badge and light switch cover on page 30 for each student. Instruct the student to use the class list to help write a sentence about conserving energy on his light switch cover as shown. Provide the student with various art supplies to decorate his badge and light switch cover. To help prevent wear and tear, laminate each student's badge and light switch cover or protect them with clear Con-Tact® paper. Have each student use a piece of double-sided tape to attach his badge to his shirt. Then encourage each energy officer to watch for energy wastefulness. To help his family remember to conserve energy, encourage each student to carefully tape his light switch cover over a light switch at home.

Turn off the light to save energy!

Down the Drain!
(Experiment)

Put in a plug for water conservation with this hands-on activity. Before lunch or snacktime, gather your students around a sink with its stopper in place. Instruct each student to wash her hands as the used water collects in the sink. After every student has washed her hands, scoop the used water into gallon jugs, using a measuring cup and a funnel to prevent spills. Have the students count the number of cups of water scooped from the sink. (Be sure not to pour the dirty water down the drain. Use it to water classroom plants.) Return to the classroom and provide each student with a copy of page 31. Instruct the student to complete the reproducible as directed. (Younger students may need assistance.) After each student completes the reproducible and colors and cuts out her pledge card, laminate the card and punch a hole in the end of the card. Place each card on a separate ring and hang the cards from a hook in the classroom where students can easily reach them. Use the pledge cards as bathroom passes and water conservation reminders.

Useful Pinwheels
(Art, Experiment)

Introduce the idea of alternative energy sources with this easy pinwheel activity. Begin by explaining to students that a windmill is a machine which operates by wind power and is used to grind grain, pump water, or generate electricity. Further explain that windmills are kind to the environment because they don't rely on fossil fuels (or other nonrenewable energy sources) for power. To make a class set of pinwheels, draw a six-inch square pattern as shown, and make a copy for each student. Then help students make their own pinwheels by reading aloud the directions below. Direct the students to hold the pinwheels by their pencil handles and take them outside to check the power of the wind for themselves.

Steps:
1. Color and cut out the square pattern.
2. Carefully cut along the dotted lines toward the center from each corner as shown.
3. Fold the marked corners to the center, securing the corners with a pushpin.
4. Slide the pushpin into the side of a pencil eraser.

Step 2

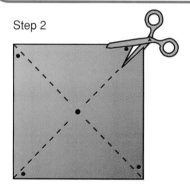

Step 3

Natural Heat
(Demonstration)

Show your youngsters the importance of color in creating solar energy with this fast-acting experiment. First, explain to students that many people in warm climates use inexpensive solar water heaters called batch heaters. These heaters create heated water by using a black tank and the sun's energy. The black tank absorbs the heat from the sun, causing the water inside it to warm up. Next, cut three pieces of tagboard (black; white; and red, yellow, or green) into four-inch squares. Position the cards in a sunny location and direct students to feel the squares as they begin to warm up. After a few minutes, put an ice cube on each square. Instruct your students to observe which cube melts the quickest. *(The ice cube on the black square will melt first, while the cube on the white square will take the longest to melt.)* Explain to students that dark colors like black absorb most of the sun's heat, while light colors like white reflect most of the sun's heat. Other colors like red, yellow, and green absorb only a small part of the sun's heat.

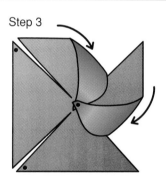

Grand Old Parks

Look at the legend below. Circle the items that can be found or the activities that can be done in a national park. Then make your own map of a pretend national park using the items you circled to help you.

Map of _____ National Park

Legend

 fishing

 camping

 rivers

 farming

 lakes

shopping mall

 bike trails

MOVIES movie theaters

wildlife viewing

schools

hiking

mountains

Be Animal Friendly

Directions for two players:
1. Put your game pieces on START.
2. Take turns rolling the die.
3. Read and follow the directions in the space you land on.
4. When both players reach "Friendly Forest," the game is over.

S T A R T

Littering on highway. Go back two spaces.

Rain forest land saved. Smile at your partner.

Ocean pollution. Make a sad face.

Wildlife preserve created. Hop in place two times.

Oil spill stopped. Go ahead two spaces.

Animal species becomes extinct. Go back to START.

Forest land cut down. Sit on your hands.

Camper's fire safely put out. Clap four times.

Water animals are tangled in fishing nets. Go back four spaces.

You have reached Friendly Forest!

Ocean pollution cleaned up. Find trash and throw it away.

Forest fire! Cover your eyes with your hands.

Oil spill! Go back three spaces.

Species of animal saved from extinction and raised in zoo. Go forward two spaces.

Clean highway. Laugh like you are happy.

Poachers kill animals for fur. Go back three spaces.

Friendly Forest

©2000 The Education Center, Inc. • Investigating Science • Environment • TEC1739

Note to the teacher: Pair students. Duplicate this page for each pair. Use with the cube on page 30.

29

Patterns

Use with "Animal Friends" on page 25.

Directions:

1. Carefully cut out the cube pattern along the outside edges.
2. Place the pattern printed side up on your desk. Fold along the uncut solid lines to form a cube. (The dots should be on the outside of the cube.)
3. Glue the tabs to the inside of the cube.

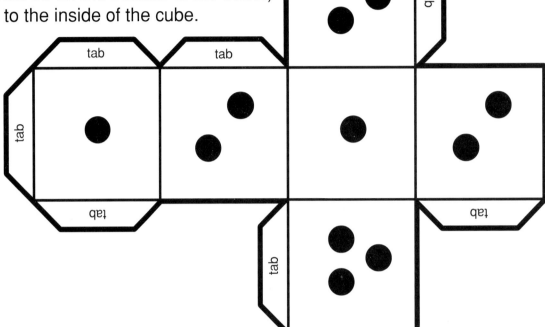

Use with "Energy Officers" on page 26.

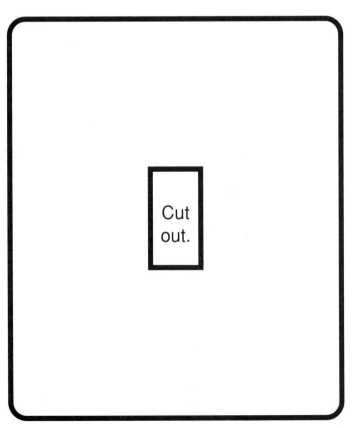

Cut out.

Name _____ *Critical thinking, graphing*

Careful Water User

Read the questions and then fill in the blanks below. Use a blue crayon to complete the water graph.

How many cups of water were used? _____

How many cups per student? _____

At this rate, how many cups would be used if each student washed his or her hands three times a day? _____

Some places and times I waste water:

1. _____

2. _____

3. _____

4. _____

5. _____

Some ways I can save water:

1. _____

2. _____

3. _____

4. _____

5. _____

Color and cut out.

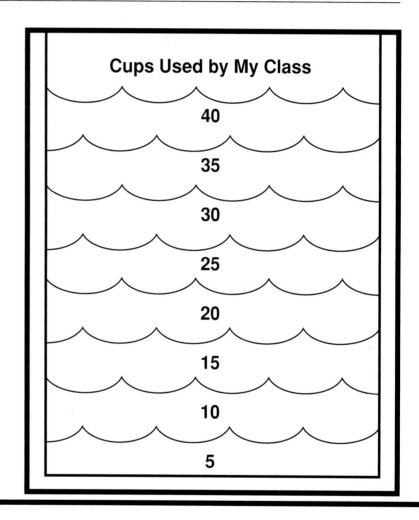

Cups Used by My Class

40

35

30

25

20

15

10

5

I pledge to be a careful water user.

_____

student's name

Pollution

Every "litter" bit of this collection of ideas will help your youngsters understand that they can't hide from pollution but must seek solutions to the environmental problems they see.

Our Pollution Solutions
(Creative Writing, Art, Bulletin Board)

Challenge students to identify pollution problems and possible solutions with this informative bulletin board. Cover half a bulletin board with bright blue paper and the other half with dull gray paper. Next, enlarge onto white construction paper the patterns on pages 38 and 39. Recruit some students to help cut out and color the patterns. Then tack the cutouts from page 38 on the blue side of the board to represent an unpolluted environment. Tack the cutouts from page 39 on the gray side to represent pollution. If desired, add some dry trash items like gum or candy wrappers to the pollution side for a 3-D effect. Title the display "Our Pollution Solutions."

Compare and contrast the two sides of the board with your class. Then invite students to share observations of pollution in their community. Point out that air, land, and water often become polluted as a result of human carelessness. Have students brainstorm possible solutions to local pollution problems. Instruct them to write about a specific pollution problem and describe a solution for it. Have students illustrate their final drafts. Then display the illustrated solutions along the outside borders of the bulletin board.

Background for the Teacher

- *Pollution* is anything not from nature that harms the environment.
- Three main types of pollution are air, water, and soil pollution.
- Fuel-burning vehicles such as cars and buses are the main causes of air pollution.
- Burning garbage in open dumps and smoke from factories also cause air pollution.
- Water covers 70% of the earth's surface. Of this water, only 3% is fresh water and only 1% is available for drinking.
- Oil spills in our oceans, lakes, rivers, and streams are particularly serious since wind, currents, and tides make cleanup difficult.
- Agricultural pesticides are one of the most hazardous forms of pollution.
- When pollutants combine with rainwater in clouds, acid rain is formed.
- Pollution also results from careless disposal of household products.

Earth-Friendly Books

The Berenstain Bears Don't Pollute (Anymore) by Stan and Jan Berenstain (Random House, 1991)

Ecology by R. Spurgeon (EDC Publications, 1990)

Oil Spill! by Melvin Berger (HarperTrophy Publishers, 1994)

Pollution and Waste by Rosie Harlow and Sally Morgan (Kingfisher Books, 1995)

Tower to the Sun by Colin Thompson (Knopf, 1997)

Our Pollution Solutions

Putting Acid to the Test
(Experiment)

Introduce your students to the dangers of acid rain and excite them with the news that they'll be testing local rainwater (collected ahead of time) and other common liquids to see which are acidic. Divide the students into small groups. Give each group the materials listed; then follow the directions below to complete the experiment. Culminate the activity by asking questions such as the following: Is our rainwater acidic? What do you think would happen if you used vinegar to water a plant? Do you think fish could live in cola?

Materials for each group:
8 paper cups labeled with the names of each liquid listed on page 36, and filled with a small amount of the appropriate liquid
8 blue litmus paper strips (available from science supply companies)
1 copy of page 36

Directions:
1. Explain that acid rain is formed as a result of air pollution and that it can poison water, harm soil, kill fish and plants, and do other damage to the environment.
2. Explain that blue litmus paper is used by scientists to test for acids and will turn red if dipped into an acid.
3. Instruct one student from each group to take a litmus strip and dip it into the rainwater cup.
4. Have the student lay his strip on the observation sheet in the corresponding box under the red column if the strip turns red or the blue column if the strip stays blue.
5. Instruct the remaining group members to repeat the process with the other liquids. Have each group compare the strips and identify the fluids that are acidic.

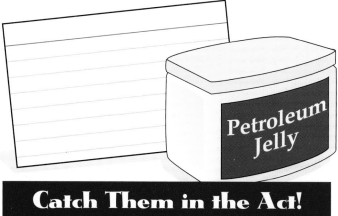

Catch Them in the Act!
(Experiment)

Catching tiny particles of air pollution at school will really be an eye-opener for your students! Provide each student with an index card. Inform your students that the index cards will be used in an experiment to see if air pollution exists in different areas of your school. On one side of the card, have each student write his name and a specific location at school where he will test for pollution. *(Indoor locations might include the classroom, cafeteria, and gym. Outside locations might include the bus-loading area, the playground, and the area just outside your classroom.)* On the other side of the card, have the student spread a layer of petroleum jelly. Explain that the petroleum jelly will "catch" the pollution. Direct each student to place his card in its assigned location. *(Students may need tape to secure their cards to a wall, chair, or other item in the chosen location.)*

After several days, have the students retrieve their cards and compare their results. Ask your students questions, such as "Did some locations produce more pollution than others?" and "Did it make a difference if the card was outside or inside?" Record their responses on chart paper. Then have each student write a brief description of the location that contained the most pollutants and an explanation of why the location may be more polluted. Your students will be wide-eyed with wonder at the pollution they hadn't noticed before.

Location	Clean	Some Pollutants	Lots of Pollutants
classroom		*	
gym		*	
playground	*		
bus-loading area			*

Thirsty Celery
(Experiment)

Here is a crunchy, healthful way for your students to discover how pollutants can get into food. Tell students that plants like celery get moisture and nutrients through their roots and stems. Explain that when polluted water is absorbed by plants, any living thing that eats the plants will also take in the pollutants. Then divide your class into pairs and guide each pair through the following experiment. Afterward, have students discuss how the celery is similar to plants on a farm being watered by polluted rainfall. *(Plants may take in pollutants along with the rain. People or animals may eat the plants, unaware of the pollutants the plants may have absorbed.)* Guide students to conclude that we must keep the earth's water clean to protect our food supply.

Materials for each group:
one 6-oz. plastic cup
apple juice
blue food coloring
1 stalk of celery with 1" cut off at the base and a slit halfway up the middle

Steps:
1. Fill each pair's cup about halfway with apple juice.
2. Add three drops of food coloring to the juice. Explain to students that the food coloring represents pollution in the water.
3. Have each student pair carefully place its celery stalk's base in the apple juice.
4. Put the cups with the celery in a place where they will not be disturbed for several hours.
5. Have students remove the celery from the cups and observe the changes that took place. *(The color will be visible from the base to the leaves.)*
6. Invite the student pairs to taste the celery. Ask the students if they can taste the apple juice. *(Even though the celery soaked up the juice, students will be unable to taste it.)*

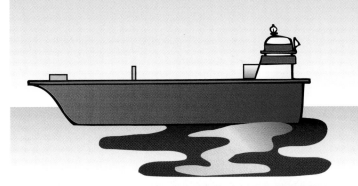

Oil and Water Don't Mix
(Experiment)

These simple activities will show your students how oil spills spoil water for marine life, birds, plants, and animals. First, read aloud *Oil Spill!* by Melvin Berger, which discusses the effects of the *Exxon Valdez* disaster. After discussing the book, divide your class into groups of four or five students. Provide each group with the materials listed; then guide each group through the steps to see that oil and water do not mix.

Materials for each group:
clear glass bowl (12 oz. or larger)
1 plastic spoon
1 drinking straw
8 oz. water
1 tbsp. vegetable oil
$1/8$ tsp. cinnamon
several small marshmallows

Steps:
1. Instruct each group to pour water into its bowl and add the vegetable oil. Guide students to observe that the water and oil don't mix.
2. Have each group sprinkle cinnamon on the oil. Point out that the mixture resembles *sludge*. Then have each group drop its marshmallows in the bowl to represent birds and animals.
3. Have one student in each group blow, first gently and then harder, on the oil through the straw. Tell students that wind and waves push the oil but the oil continues to float on the surface.
4. Have each group observe the marshmallows and the interior sides of the bowl. Point out that a layer of oil coats the marshmallows and the side of the bowl as crude oil would coat the ocean's shoreline and wildlife.
5. Direct each group to skim the oil from the water with the spoon. Then discuss the difficulty of removing the oil from the water.

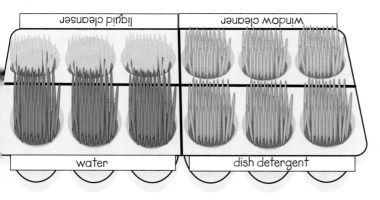

water | liquid cleanser
window cleaner | dish detergent

Keep off the Grass
(Experiment)

Did you know that the products you use to clean your dishes, clothes, and home may be dangerous to living things in our environment? Help students compare the effects of safe and unsafe household cleaning products on the environment. Gather the following supplies ahead of time and carefully mix each pair of liquids with one part cleaner to three parts water: liquid commercial cleanser and water, window cleaner and water, and liquid dish-washing detergent and water. Next, for each group of three or four students, label three clean, empty bottles, each with one of the solutions. Label a fourth bottle "water." Then fill each bottle with the appropriate solution or water. Guide each group through the following steps to complete the experiment. Supervise students closely as they work with these potentially harmful solutions. At the completion of the experiment, have each group share how the seedlings were affected by the different solutions.

Materials for each group:
4 clean plastic 20-oz. soda bottles, 1 styrofoam® egg carton, potting soil, grass seeds, window cleaner, dishwashing liquid, liquid commercial cleanser, water

Directions:
1. Use a black marker to divide the egg carton into fourths as shown. Label each section with a different solution name or "water."
2. Fill each section of the egg carton with potting soil and sprinkle grass seed in each cup.
3. Water the seeds with tap water each day keeping the soil moist. The grass will begin to sprout in seven to ten days.
4. When the grass is about one-quarter inch high, begin using the three solutions to water the appropriate sections. Continue watering the fourth section with tap water.
5. Check your seedlings each day and record your observations in science journals.
6. After two weeks, compare your results with another group.

Environmentally Friendly Cleaners
(Experiment)

Introduce your students to earth-friendly alternatives to harmful cleaning products with these two simple recipes for environmentally safe window and all-purpose cleaners. Divide students into groups of three or four, and provide each group with the recipes and the materials listed. Direct each group to follow the recipes to prepare these nature-safe solutions. Then have each group name its new cleaning products and design advertising posters promoting their many advantages. Display the finished posters along the hall. Allow time for students to experiment with their cleansers by cleaning desks, tabletops, and windows in your classroom. Once your classroom is sparkling clean, give students copies of the recipes and encourage them to share their pollution solutions with their own families.

Window Cleaner:

Ingredients/Supplies:
2 tbsp. vinegar
16 oz. water
large spray bottle
Directions:
Combine the vinegar and water in a spray bottle. Shake gently to blend.

All-Purpose Cleaner:

Ingredients/Supplies:
1½ tsp. castile soap (available at health food stores)
1 tbsp. vinegar
16 oz. water
large spray bottle
Directions:
Combine soap, vinegar, and water in a spray bottle. Shake gently to blend.

Window Cleaner

All-Purpose Cleaner

Putting Acid to the Test

Liquid	Red	Blue
rain		
apple juice		
milk of magnesia		
vinegar		
cola		
baking soda mixed with tap water		
lemon juice		
milk		

Note to the teacher: Use with "Putting Acid to the Test" on page 33. For baking soda solution: Add one teaspoon of baking soda to a jar half-filled with water, and mix.

Be a Pollution Problem Solver

Directions: Solve each problem, using the space to show your work. Write your answer in the box at the right. Then read the amazing pollution facts!

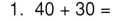

1. 40 + 30 =

2. 56 – 32 =

3. 24 + 12 =

4. 11 – 1 =

5. 100 + 40 =

6. 22 – 11 =

7. 7 – 3 =

8. 30 + 30 =

9. 8 + 8 =

1. Every day in the United States, an average of ☐ gallons of water is used by each person.

2. A person taking a two-minute shower uses ☐ gallons of water.

3. ☐ thousand dead birds were found within the first few weeks after a ship in Alaska spilled 10,567,000 gallons of oil into the sea.

4. One out of every ☐ streams, lakes, and rivers in the United States is polluted with metals and toxic chemicals.

5. All life on earth depends on the oceans, which cover almost ☐ square miles of the earth's surface.

6. People who change their own car oil dump ☐ million gallons of oil onto the land every three weeks.

7. Each person in the United States throws away three to ☐ pounds of garbage each day!

8. More than ☐ million tons of paper and cardboard are thrown away each year.

9. Each year we throw away more than ☐ billion diapers.

Patterns

Use with "Our Pollution Solutions" on page 32.

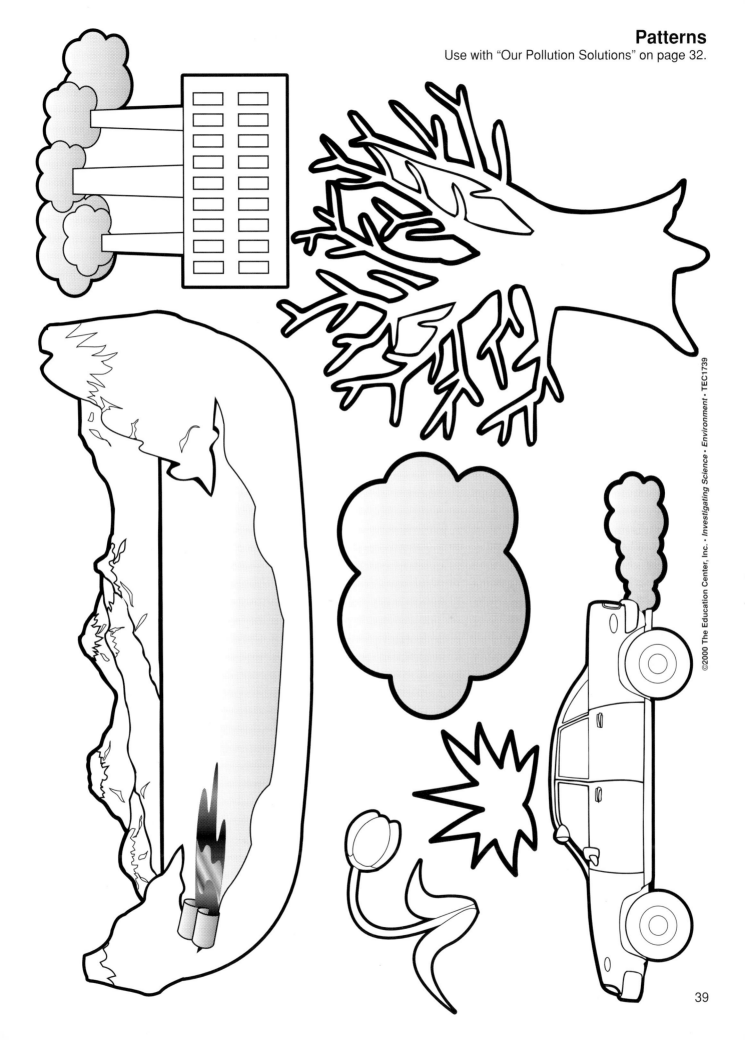

Changes in the Environment

Explore changes in the environment, both man-made and nature-made, with this set of activities, experiments, and reproducibles.

Background for the Teacher

- Some scientists believe that the use of fossil fuels is the cause of increased carbon dioxide levels in our atmosphere.
- Earth's atmosphere acts like a greenhouse retaining energy from the Sun.
- Global temperatures are expected to continue to rise, and, as a result, sea level will rise and precipitation and local climate conditions will change.
- Globally, sea level has risen four to ten inches over the past one hundred years.
- Loss of trees, plants, and other vegetation can result in erosion, floods, and avalanches.
- As a result of the *Exxon Valdez* oil spill on March 24, 1989, over 300,000 ducks, geese, and seabirds died.
- When acid rain comes in contact with marble and limestone, a crumbling substance called *gypsum* is created, and buildings and statues corrode.

Meltdown
(Experiment)

Give students a peek at global warming in action with this icy activity. Prepare for the lesson by gathering eight empty margarine tubs. Fill each tub with water and freeze. Keep the water frozen until it is time for the experiment.

Divide the class into eight groups. Give each group an empty pie pan, a ruler, and a pitcher of water. Have one member of the group stand the ruler in the pie pan while another member pours water into the pan until it reaches the half-inch mark on the ruler. Next, distribute one frozen tub to each group. Explain to the children that the water in the pan represents the ocean and the ice represents an iceberg. Direct the group to place the tub upside down in the water and gently squeeze the sides so that the ice falls from the tub into the water. Collect the tubs; then place each group's pie pan in a safe spot for four to five hours and allow the ice to melt. Instruct each group to measure the new water level in its pie pan. Discuss the results with the class. Guide students into understanding that the water level rises as the ice melts. Point out that the level of the ocean could also rise if global warming caused snow on mountains and land to melt. This water would eventually end up in the streams and rivers that dump into the oceans.

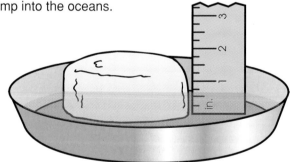

I'm a Little Iceberg
(Song)

Demonstrate the movements for this song; then ask students to sing with you!

(sung to the tune of "I'm a Little Teapot")

I'm a little iceberg	*Raise arms out to shoulder level.*
In the sea.	*Sway side to side with arms outstretched.*
See the peak of snow	*Pat top of head.*
That sits on me.	*Point to self.*
When the sun shines on me,	*Round arms above head.*
I will be	*Droop as if melting.*
Melting slowly into the sea!	*Sit on the floor.*

Reading About the Environment

Cloudy With a Chance of Meatballs by Judi Barrett (Aladdin Paperbacks, 1982)

Oil Spill! (Let's Read-and-Find-Out Science, Stage 2) by Melvin Berger (HarperTrophy, 1994)

River Ran Wild: An Environmental History by Lynne Cherry (Houghton Mifflin, 1995)

Closer Look at Volcanoes by Jen Green (Copper Beech Books, 1998)

Fade-Out
(Experiment, Critical Thinking)

Use the following experiment to shed some light on the damaging effects of the Sun. In advance, create a window by drawing four 4" x 7" rectangular panes on a 12" x 18" sheet of white construction paper as shown. Next, cut out three of the panes. Then tape a sheet of clear plastic wrap over each opening. Purchase two bottles of sunscreen lotion with different SPF ratings.

Have a student apply an even, thin layer of lotion to one of the window-panes. Instruct another student to apply a layer of the second lotion to a different windowpane. Next, place a piece of newspaper in a spot, prefer-ably outside, that receives direct sunlight. Lay the window on top of the newspaper and tape it in place. If the window is placed outside, put small rocks or bricks on each corner to weigh it down. Leave the window in place for two school days. *(Bring the window indoors at the end of each day to prevent rain or morning dew from damaging the experiment.)*

Carefully lift the window from the newspaper. Discuss with your stu-dents any changes observed in the color of the newspaper. Then place the window back on the newspaper in exactly the same position. Leave it in the sunlight for two more school days.

Remove the window from the newspaper a second time and ask the class to discuss the changes observed after two days. Talk about how the different strengths of sunscreen may have affected the amount of fading on the newspaper. Compare these changes to the newspaper area beneath the pane with no sunscreen and the newspaper area beneath the uncut pane.

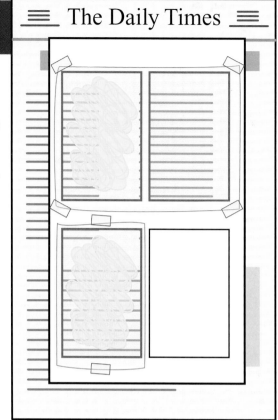

The Daily Times

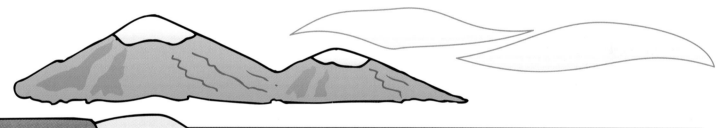

Acid Rain
(Experiment)

Acid rain damage can be easily demonstrated with a piece of chalk and a cup of vinegar. Divide the class into groups of three or four. Give each group a stick of white chalk, an eyedropper, a clean cup, a cup of vinegar, and a sheet of paper. Direct the group to write a description or draw a picture of the chalk on the paper. Then instruct the group to place the chalk in the clean cup. Ask one member of the group to squeeze an eyedropper full of vinegar on the chalk. Have the group discuss the changes that occur before they write a description or draw a picture of the changes observed. Provide time for each group to share its results with the class. Explain to students that acid rain can damage statues, bridges, and buildings in the same way that the vinegar damaged the chalk.

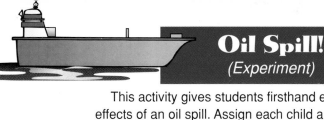

Oil Spill!
(Experiment)

This activity gives students firsthand experience with the effects of an oil spill. Assign each child a partner. Provide a copy of page 45 for each twosome. Ask the children to imagine that an actual oil spill has occurred and that they have been assigned to determine the best method to clean the birds that are coated with oil. To complete the activity, each pair of children will need a feather, several cotton balls, a dish of cooking oil, a dish of dishwashing detergent, and a dish of water. Have each child work with his partner to complete the steps of the experiment. Once each twosome has completed the sheet, gather the students and discuss the experiment and their findings. Ask the class to discuss possible methods that volunteers can use to clean birds that are in real oil spills.

Greenhouse Effect
(Demonstration)

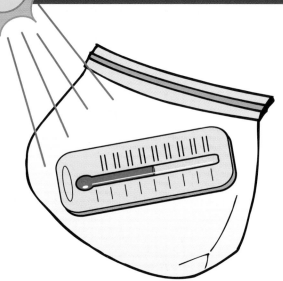

Perform this experiment outside on a sunny day to help students understand the greenhouse effect. Have the children sit in a circle on the playground. Place a thermometer in the center of the circle. After five minutes have passed, check the temperature and have one student record it on a sheet of paper. Next, drop a thermometer into a gallon-size, resealable plastic bag. Then gently blow up the bag and seal it tightly. Leave the bag in the center of the circle for five minutes before checking the temperature. Have a different student record the temperature on the sheet of paper. Explain to students that the layer of plastic will retain the energy from the sun inside the bag and make the temperature rise. Further explain that, similarly, the gases in Earth's atmosphere retain the Sun's energy and cause Earth's temperature to rise.

Rain Forest on a Stick
(Cooking)

Can you imagine a world without chocolate? The world's rain forests are being destroyed at alarming rates. In fact, an area the size of a football field is being destroyed every second! Many of the foods that we enjoy are found in the rain forest. For a tasty treat made from rain forest products, have your students create these banana snacks! Instruct each student to carefully push a craft stick into the cut end of a peeled banana half. Next, have her roll the banana in Hershey's® chocolate syrup. Then, roll the banana in shredded coconut, chopped peanuts, or chopped cashew nuts. Enjoy!

Erosion
(Experiment)

When trees are cut down, the soil around them has a greater chance of eroding. Use the following experiment to demonstrate this process for your students. In advance, divide the class into groups of four. Supply each group with the materials listed below; then have students follow the directions below to complete the experiment. At the conclusion of the experiment, have each group discuss its findings with the class.

Materials needed for each group:

2 shallow pans
grass seed
potting soil
watering can filled with water
marker

Directions:

1. Fill the pans with potting soil. Label one pan "soil" and the other pan "seed." Plant the grass seed in rows in the pan labeled "seed." Water both pans lightly.
2. Place the pans side by side with one end of each pan resting on a stack of books so that the end is elevated four inches. Allow the grass seed to grow until it is two inches high (approximately three days).
3. Use the watering can to make it "rain" on the two pans. The topsoil in the pan with no grass will be swept down to the bottom of the pan. The topsoil in the pan with the grass will be held in place by the grass and its roots.

The Wumps' World
(Literature, Sequencing, Recalling Events)

The Wump World by Bill Peet (Houghton Mifflin Company, 1981) tells the story of a planet that changes from a peaceful, beautiful world to a chaotic, polluted mess. The Wumps' story helps students understand what changes in the environment can do to a planet. After reading the book aloud, have each child trace a circle template onto a sheet of white construction paper and cut it out. Then ask him to color the cutout to resemble the Wumps' planet. Next, provide a copy of page 46 for each student and instruct the child to cut out the booklet pages on the bold lines. Have him personalize the front page and then sequentially stack the booklet pages. Direct him to staple the pages at the top and then glue the back of the last booklet page to the front of his planet cutout as shown. Instruct the child to draw and color a picture on each booklet page to match the sentence on that page. Display the completed booklets on a bulletin board titled "The Wumps' World."

The Wumps' World

Trysten
Name

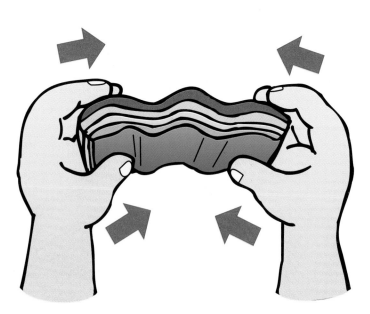

Pushing and Shifting
(Experiment)

Use the following experiment to show students that not all changes in the environment are caused by man—some are caused by nature. Gather a class supply of four different colors of modeling clay, a roll of waxed paper, and rolling pins. Next, tell your students that all of the world's highest mountain ranges, including the Alps and the Rocky Mountains, are called *fold* mountains because they were formed when two plates of the earth's crust were pushed into each other, causing the land in between to buckle and fold. Then give each student four different-colored balls of modeling clay (each about the size of a golf ball) and a sheet of waxed paper. Have the child use a rolling pin to roll out each ball of clay into a flat piece. Next, direct the student to stack the flat pieces of clay on the sheet of waxed paper and press them together to represent the different rock layers of the earth's crust. Then have the child place one hand on each side of the clay and push each end toward the middle. *(The clay will buckle and fold and form hills and mountains.)* Tell your students that they've just created mountains!

I Predict...
(Critical Thinking, Making Predictions, Creative Writing)

Wrap up your study of the environment by having students make their own predictions about the future of the planet. Give each child a copy of page 47. Have the child keep in mind what she has learned about the changes in the environment as she writes a story describing her predictions for the future. Provide time for each child to share her story with the class; then bind the completed pages into a book titled "I Predict…"

I Predict...

Name James

I belive that the future looks good for our planet because...

Name _____ *Experiment*

Oil Spill!

1. How does the feather look and feel? _____
_____
_____

Draw a picture of it.

2. Dip a cotton ball in the oil and gently wipe the oil on the feather. How does the feather look and feel?
_____
_____

Draw a picture of it.

3. Dip a clean cotton ball in the water and try to wipe the oil off the feather. What happens? _____
_____
_____

Draw a picture of it.

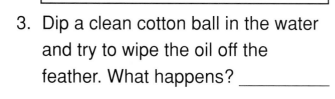

4. Dip a clean cotton ball in the detergent and try to wipe the oil off the feather. Dip the feather in the water. What happens? _____
_____
_____

Draw a picture of it.

The Wumps' World

_____
Name

Factories fill the air with smog. The water is polluted. The Pollutians are unhappy.

The Pollutians board their space-ships and leave the planet.

The Wumps enjoy life on their beautiful planet.

The Pollutians arrive and claim the Wumps' planet.

The Wumps resume life on the planet, but it is never the same.

I Predict...

Name _____

Page 21

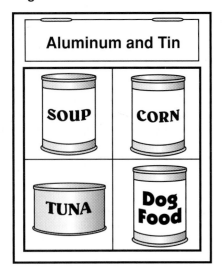

Page 28

The following should be circled:
fishing
camping
rivers
lakes
bike trails
wildlife viewing
hiking
mountains

Each student's map design will vary.

Page 37

1. 70
2. 24
3. 36
4. 10
5. 140
6. 11
7. 4
8. 60
9. 16

Page 36

rain—answer may vary
apple juice—red
milk of magnesia—blue
vinegar—red
cola—red (may appear a light or pale red)
baking soda mixed with tap water—blue
lemon juice—red
milk—blue